PHILIP
PULLMAN

AUTHORS TEENS LOVE

Philip Pullman

Master of Fantasy

Susan E. Reichard

Enslow Publishers, Inc.
40 Industrial Road
Box 398
Berkeley Heights, NJ 07922
USA

http://www.enslow.com

To my life support system:
Dave
Sarah Joy
Rebecca
Jennifer
Dave, Jr.

Copyright © 2006 by Susan E. Reichard

Library of Congress Cataloging-in-Publication Data

Reichard, Susan E.
    Philip Pullman : master of fantasy / Susan E. Reichard.
       p. cm. — (Authors teens love)
    Includes bibliographical references and index.
    ISBN 0-7660-2447-4
    1. Pullman, Philip, 1946—-Juvenile literature. 2. Authors, English—
20th century—Biography—Juvenile literature. 3. Young adult fiction,
English—History and criticism—Juvenile literature. 4. Fantasy fiction,
English—History and criticism—Juvenile literature. I. Title. II. Series.
    PR6066.U44Z85 2006
    823'.914—dc22

                                2005029825

Printed in the United States of America

10 9 8 7 6 5 4 3 2 1

Illustration Credits: AP/Wide World Photos, p. 57; Everett Collection,
Inc., p. 66; Oxford University. p. 21; Courtesy of Philip Pullman,
pp. 6, 26, 39, 47, 50, 70, 73.

Cover Illustration: Courtesy of Philip Pullman (foreground); AP/Wide
World Photos (background).

CONTENTS

CHAPTER 1

SERVANT OF THE STORY

The telegram arrived late in the day when Philip and his younger brother, Francis, were playing in back of his grandparents' home, pulling moss from a stone wall. What had begun as a beautiful day for young Philip soon turned dark and tragic. His mother was visibly upset. He could see she had been crying about something. His grandmother explained that a telegram had arrived from Africa telling that his father had been killed when his plane had been shot down by terrorists in a far-away country. Philip was only six, but his life was forever changed.[1]

Fans of Philip Pullman's books know that most of his stories have an absent father or no father at all. Lyra Belacqua's father in *The Golden Compass* is unknown to her. Will Parry's father in *The Subtle Knife* is also missing from his life. The father of

Sally Lockhart, the young detective in Pullman's mystery series, has also recently died. This life-changing event of losing his father at a young age has played a role in most of Pullman's stories. This tragedy from his childhood and his commitment to tell the truth in his stories are important features of his writing.

Pullman's fans know by heart the first line from his award-winning book *The Golden Compass*: "Lyra and her daemon moved through the darkening hall, taking care to keep to one side, out of the sight of the kitchen." With these simple words Philip Pullman opened an epic story that is loved by teens and adults alike. Once a beloved teacher, his writing has made him a Commander of the British Empire, an honor bestowed on him by Queen Elizabeth II of Great Britain in 2004.[2]

But his writing has also caused him great trouble, especially with some religious groups. Pullman is the man who "killed god" in *The Amber Spyglass*. Many people think he has committed heresy in his books. Yet Pullman never hides from the truth as he sees it. He is proud to discuss his own beliefs and how these beliefs are reflected in his books.

Pullman's journey from unknown writer to worldwide celebrity has taken place over thirty years. Writer Terence Blacker has said that Pullman's trilogy, also known as *His Dark Materials*, is "a genuine masterpiece of intelligent, imaginative storytelling." Critics have suggested that Pullman may be "the best storyteller ever."[3]

Pullman's trilogy (*The Golden Compass*, *The Subtle Knife*, and *The Amber Spyglass*) is based on John Milton's classic work, *Paradise Lost*, published in 1667. It tells the Genesis story from the Bible: how Adam and Eve were created and how they lost their place in the Garden of Eden. Pullman's three volumes have won many awards and have sold more than 7 million copies in Britain and the United States alone. The books have also been translated into thirty-seven languages.[4]

Common themes run throughout Pullman's books. These "lessons," as he calls them, develop from the story itself. Some of these themes are revealed through the strong female characters he creates. Lyra Belacqua, Mrs. Coulter, Serafina Pekkala, Mary Malone, and Sally Lockhart are strong-willed and courageous. They desire to better themselves and their worlds and they inspire others to be the best they can be. Other themes found in Pullman's books include the battle of good versus evil, the end of innocence, and the beginning of wisdom. His characters grow and mature through their adventures as they make discoveries about life along the way. Pullman also believes that hope and optimism and finding joy in this life on Earth are critical themes in his books.

Readers are usually surprised to discover that Pullman's favorite character is the evil and devious Mrs. Coulter, Lyra's mother from the *His Dark Materials* trilogy.[5] Perhaps Mrs. Coulter reminds him of his own mother, who had to leave her boys with their grandparents after her husband died.

She moved to London to earn a living to support the family.

Pullman's grandfather was influential in developing Philip's gift for telling stories. His grandfather was a kind and compassionate man. He was also the pastor (or church leader) of his village. He was beloved in his community and he provided love and support for his grandsons, especially after the death of their father.

> ## "Each night when the lights went out, I would tell . . . a story that I made up as I went along."
> ### —Philip Pullman

Pullman's first attempts at storytelling began when he and his younger brother would go to bed. "Each night when the lights went out, I would tell [Francis] a story that I made up as I went along. I do not know if he enjoyed it or if he even listened, but it was not for his benefit, but for mine. I remember vividly the sense of diving into the dark as I began the story with absolutely no idea at all of what was going to happen or whether the story would come out as I intended."[6]

Pullman's stories must have come out as he intended. His success as a writer has earned him many awards, including the Whitbread Award, the British Carnegie Medal awarded for the best in children's literature, and the Guardian Children's Award, which he received in 1994 and 1996.

For many years Pullman has written his amazing stories in a quaint potting shed in the back of the garden behind a house in Oxford, England. The shed is his "nest." In his silent 12-foot-by-eight-foot wooden refuge, armored bears, harpies, and witches came to life. Pullman sits in a very expensive Danish orthopedic swivel chair to create his worlds. Apple cores, spiders' webs, dust, books for him to review, and a thousand plastic bags are his shedmates. His six-foot-long stuffed rat is a "character" from a production of a Sherlock Holmes play Pullman wrote for the Polka Children's Theatre. As Pullman asserts, "no one would go in there unless they absolutely had to."[7]

Throughout his long writing career, Pullman has collected interesting memorabilia from around the world. This collection has shared space with him in his writing shed. He is reluctant to throw anything out because it might bring him bad luck. He once shared his writing space with a guitar, saxophone, and gaudy artificial flowers. From his former life as a school teacher, he has collected masks designed and created for many plays he wrote for his students to perform. Also among the ruin and rubble are a bit of chewed carpet from when his young pug Hogarth visited, and stones of all kinds, including a cobblestone from Prague, a stone from Cape Cod in Massachusetts, and a piece from Mont Blanc in France, the highest mountain in Western Europe.[8]

Philip Pullman believes in being true to the story no matter where it leads. This honesty in his writing has made his books controversial and troublesome to some people. He insists that his responsibility as a storyteller is to tell the truth. Pullman also believes that a story is given to the writer. It must be looked after and protected.

> Because the story knows what it wants to be and what it must be, the writer must go in this direction and just say to the story, "ok, you're the boss." This is the point where responsibility takes the form of service, not servitude, not shameful toil, but service, freely and fairly entered into. As the servant, I have to do what a good servant should. I have to be ready to attend to my work at a regular time each day. I have to anticipate where the story wants to go and find out what can make the progress easier by doing research, spending time in libraries, by going to talk to people, and by finding things out. I have to keep myself sober and in good health. A writer cannot serve two masters. I must be the "servant of the story."[9]

Some people believe that Pullman's books represent an evil and this evil is an element that must be silenced. The path of truth remains the only way for Philip, who is truly the "servant of the story."

CHAPTER 2

STORYTELLING SEEDS

Philip Pullman was born in Norwich, England, on October 19, 1946. His father was in the Royal Air Force and his mother dutifully followed her husband from station to station with their two small boys. The Pullmans were living in Africa, in what is now called Zimbabwe, in 1953.

When Mrs. Pullman and the boys were on a home visit to England, the sad telegram arrived informing them that Mr. Pullman had been shot down and killed. He was awarded the Distinguished Flying Cross medal by Queen Elizabeth II. This award is presented to the families of pilots who accomplish brave deeds during a flight. Mrs. Pullman and the two boys traveled to Buckingham Palace, the home of the Queen in

London. There, Philip's mother received the medal in a private ceremony.[1]

When Philip was young, he attended a school that was rumored to be haunted. Every student knew the ghost story: One day a boy walked to the principal's office and opened the door. The principal slammed the door shut on the boy's wrist, cutting off his hand. The boy bled to death and had haunted the school ever since.[2]

Philip was glad to leave that school, but ghost stories became his favorite kind of stories. Philip used to enjoy scaring his friends with the ghost tales he read. He also liked to make up stories about a tree in the woods that he and his friends called the Hanging Tree. They were terrified of this tree and imagined that eerie creatures lived and lurked among its heavy branches.[3]

After their father's death, Philip and his younger brother continued to live with their grandparents. This was a big change, but it was the time in Philip's young life when the first seeds of storytelling were planted. Their mother was then working for the British Broadcasting Company. This is the government-run radio and television service in England.

Philip's grandfather became the center of his life and the biggest influence on him. He was a widely respected member of the village. People were always stopping by to visit. Philip thought his grandfather was the kindest and wisest person. What Philip loved more than anything else about his grandfather was that he told stories.

Philip attended church and Sunday School regularly during the years he lived with his grandparents. His grandfather's influence was so important that even today Philip measures what he writes against his grandfather's judgment and whether he would approve of the stories. His grandmother was an equally kind woman. Philip was sad when he and his brother had to leave this home where they received unconditional love.[4]

Ghost stories became Philip's favorite kind of stories.

When Philip was nine, his mother remarried. A man he had called "Uncle" Johnny now became his father. Like Philip's biological father, he was also a pilot in the Royal Air Force. This meant more travel for Philip and his brother. Their next trip was a sea voyage to Australia.

Philip enjoyed these long sea voyages on the great ocean liners. There was always wonderful food aboard the ships and it was available at all hours of the day. There were cakes and pastries that would melt in your mouth, luscious ice cream in every flavor, and huge dinners every evening in a big dining room that sparkled with chandeliers of light. Philip also loved to watch the ocean. One day there might be so many different types of waves to watch and the next day the ocean might be as flat as a pancake.

Journeys by sea often take several weeks and this is how Philip came to be a great observer of the ocean. He loved the way the weather changed when the ship left the colder Northern Hemisphere and entered the warmer Southern Hemisphere. The greatest fun on a voyage was when the ship crossed the Equator. This was known as "crossing the Line" and was always a special occasion. King Neptune would visit with all of his mermaids and set up his court by the ship's pool. Passengers who had never before "crossed the Line," were initiated by being dunked in the pool. The men would also be "shaved" using a bucket of foam and a huge wooden razor.

Philip also made another discovery on this voyage to Australia. He discovered girls. Somewhere in the Indian Ocean, Philip played Postman's Knock (similar to the American game of Spin the Bottle) with some other equally curious children. Philip kissed a young girl and immediately fell madly in love with her. But, as luck would have it, she went her way and Philip went his way and that ended their shipboard romance.

Philip was on his way to Australia. A new continent and a new country lay ahead. He was used to these changes—a new school and new friends—but he had no idea that in this new place, with a new father, the seeds to his future as a storyteller would be planted.

CHAPTER 3

COMIC BOOKS AND SUPERHEROES

Nine-year-old Philip Pullman loved Australia. He lived there when television had not yet come to that part of the world, so Philip would pass the time listening to the radio dramas that were very popular. He loved the "Adventures of Superman." He also began a lifelong love of comic books.

Philip had always been a reader, but a Superman comic book given to him by his step-father changed his life. He could not get enough of these wonderful stories told also in pictures. Philip also now had the problem of convincing his parents that these comics really were "proper" to read.

Philip adored Superman, Captain America, Dick Tracy, and Batman. Philip loved this unique way of telling a story through pictures. The comics were delivered in the newspapers. The newspaper boy would ride down the street and throw the papers into the yards of subscribers. Each week Philip would anxiously await the paper with his comics. He would run out to pick the paper up as soon as it arrived. He still remembers this excitement he felt.[1]

Philip and his younger brother, Francis, shared a bedroom. Each night before drifting off to sleep, Philip would entertain his brother with made-up stories. Sometimes they would be about his favorite superhero but mostly they would be made-up stories with neither Philip nor his brother knowing quite well how the story would end. There was a kangaroo that kept tools in his pouch who would be a character in many of Philip's stories. He loved the way a story would come together and was excited when all of the parts of the story fit properly. These early tales helped Philip learn the craft of storytelling.

Philip's time in Australia ended quickly and the next year, at age ten, Philip was living back in England. His stepfather retired from the Royal Air Force and was now home with his growing family. In addition to his brother Francis, Philip now had a new brother and a new sister.

The family moved to northern Wales, a part of Great Britain located west of England, where Philip and his friends roamed the hills and countryside for hours every day. There were miles of beach to explore and when it was hot they swam in the ocean. He made go-carts and drove them down the hills, and placed pennies on the railway tracks to make them flat and shiny after the train passed over them. Philip and his friends held spitting contests and put fireworks in the ladies' toilets. He would not recommend any of these activities for youngsters today.

During this time Philip had an experience he would never forget. He was walking home from school when a man on a motorcycle drove by. A few minutes later the man came back to tell Philip that there was a dead man lying in the road up ahead and that he would be phoning for help. Philip knew at that moment he had a choice to make: Would he go the regular way home, or would he go a different way to avoid seeing the dead man? After some thought, he decided to go see the dead man. After all, he might never have another chance like this again. He approached the man, who looked as if he were peacefully sleeping on the grass. He was a bit disappointed at the sight.[2]

Philip loved this time spent living in Wales. It was the longest time he and his family had stayed in any one place. In his free time, he loved to read and to write poetry. After buying a book called *The History of Art*, he began to draw obsessively. He drew the beautiful landscapes and scenery of Wales, including stone walls, beaches, old homes, and churches. Philip's English teacher, Enid Jones, provided encouragement and support to him as he continued to write poetry. He began to memorize his favorite poems and, for a while, believed he would become a poet. Philip later changed his mind and set his sights on becoming an English teacher.[3]

Philip decided to apply to Oxford University, a very prestigious college in England. He would be the first person in his family to go to university, and so it was a great honor for Philip when he received a scholarship to attend Oxford University. Philip started his studies at Exeter College (a college within the Oxford University system) with

He began to memorize his favorite poems and, for awhile, believed he would become a poet.

great enthusiasm and was eager to learn the proper way to write. He was disappointed with the teaching and the lack of support he received there. It was at Oxford, though, that Philip realized he would be a storyteller. This was his new passion. He started by buying a large composition book in which to write a novel. He decided he would write at least three pages each day but, after a time, Philip lost interest in this story and never even typed it up.

He did not forget the beauty and mystery of Exeter College, and used this historic institution as the setting for the beginning of what would become one of his most famous books, *The Golden Compass*.[4] Although Philip changed the name of

The front quad of Exeter College at Oxford University in England.

his college from Exeter College to Jordan College, this is where his famous character Lyra Belaqua hides behind the armchair in the Retiring Room and sees the Master pouring white powder into someone's drink.

Pullman remembered the mists from the nearby river creating a ominous feeling around the ivy-covered college which also lent an air of mystery and intrigue.

Disappointed by his studies and poor grades in college, Philip soon lost interest in his desire to write his novel. His plans to write a book and become a very rich and famous man soon faded. He knew he had to find a way to make a living.

CHAPTER 4

THE STORYTELLING TEACHER

Philip Pullman decided to move to the big city of London, where he found a job working in a men's formal clothing shop. He did not like his job, but he certainly enjoyed the unique and interesting people who worked with him. Some of them were unemployed actors waiting for parts on television or in the theater. Some were poets and painters, and quite a few were people from all over the world, just passing through on their way to other countries to pursue their dreams.[1]

Each day on his lunch hour, Pullman walked to a nearby churchyard to write. He also worked on his novel after work. Soon Pullman decided to find a new job. He was fond of the people he worked with, but he was ready for something different. He found work as a school librarian. Philip enjoyed this job, especially the discovery of books that were written for young people. Some of these books included topics considered controversial by some parents. Pullman invited six parents from the school to read some of these books. They agreed that while the topics might have been controversial, the authors had written about them in a suitable and appropriate manner and, therefore, the books should be included in the school library. Pullman was happy that the parents had accepted these books and the topics they dealt with. It told him that he, too, could write for young people truthfully. It made him realize that he just might want to write stories for this audience.[2]

Pullman enjoyed his time as school librarian, but if he wanted to stay on he would have to become certified as a librarian. He decided teaching might be a good profession, so he entered Weymouth College for one year and became certified as a teacher. He saw an advertisement for a teaching job in the town of Oxford. He applied for the position and was happy to get it.

He moved himself and his new wife (he married Judith Speller in 1970) to Oxford to begin his new teaching job. Philip and his wife still live in Oxford today. They have two sons: Jamie was born in 1971 and Tom in 1982. Pullman's first novel, *The Haunted Storm*, was published in 1972. It is a book he is not happy with today and he does not discuss it.[3]

Pullman's students in Oxford were around twelve years old. Teaching helped him to learn how to tell stories. He decided that his students should learn about Greek mythology. He located several books that contained exciting retellings and he began to tell his students these ancient stories about the gods, goddesses, heroes, and mythical creatures.

Pullman did not just read these stories—he learned them by heart and told his students about Jason and his Golden Fleece. He told them about the adventures of Hercules and the legends written by Homer. Pullman brought these characters to life for his students. He prepared a course that would run for one year. He would start the year with the births and origins of these mythic characters and tell about their traits and adventures. In the second term he would tell the stories of the Trojan War and the *Iliad* and the *Odyssey*.

Telling these stories over and over taught Pullman about the rhythm and timing of the words. It taught him to consider his audience and to appreciate that the timing of events in a story is very important. Pullman learned how to bring a scene to life and make the listener and readers of his stories beg to know what happens next. Pullman still has these stories memorized and uses them from time to time.

Once, while on a family vacation, Pullman used one of his stories to entertain his young son. They were waiting for their meal in a restaurant and the boy was having trouble sitting and waiting patiently to be served. Pullman decided to tell a story from the *Odyssey*. His son was so engaged in listening

Philip Pullman is pictured here around the time he began teaching middle-schoolers in Oxford.

that when Pullman came to one especially exciting part, the boy bit a chunk out of the glass of water that he had been drinking. This caused the waitress to drop their tray of food, which in turn caused a huge commotion throughout the restaurant.[4]

As a teacher, Pullman was also placed in charge of the drama department at his school. This meant being responsible for performing a play with the students each year. Pullman decided to try his hand at writing a play for his students to perform. His first play was *Count Karlstein*. The students loved the play and it was a big hit. Pullman later turned this play into a novel that was published in 1982. Each year he would add a new theatrical trick to his plays. One year he thought fireworks would be a fun and exciting addition to the performance. *The Firework-Maker's Daughter* was born.

Greta Stoddart, an award-winning British poet, is a former student of Pullman's. She attended Bishop Kirk Middle School in Oxford from 1976–79. She fondly remembered her years with Pullman, stating:

> My most vivid memory is of him storming into the classroom. Storming being the operative word. There was always something a bit wild and elemental about him. As if the wind had blown him into our quiet Oxford School. He had long wavy hair and he would run his fingers through it rather dramatically. . . . I was in his guitar lessons too, where it felt like all that wild energy would still as he'd cradle the instrument, close his eyes and play some sad and lovely tune. He never had books with him. Everything was in his head. He would come in, his

booming voice already starting in on some story, introducing the cast list of some ancient myth. He was wild about myths and spoke about Zeus or Poseidon as if they were people he knew, and with passion. Stories were his life. Imagining things. Making things up. . . . Once he got us going on a project where we had to make up a city—we called it Vladisvok—and we each had to create our own part of it. I created the Vladisvok Opera House. Someone else its Palace and Important Persons and its big wide river. At the end of a few weeks we had built, through drawings and writing our very own city. I remember feeling amazed that we had all brought this place to life from nothing. It was ours.[5]

Theater was another passion of Philip Pullman. Every year he would write a play for the fourth-year students (twelve to thirteen year olds). One year the play was *Spring-Heeled Jack*. As Stoddart also recalled:

Mr. Pullman's imagination appeared limitless and in some way felt like his nourishment. He was different from other teachers because of his energy and boldness, his straight-talking and his unstoppable creativity, his genuine love of telling stories and stirring our imaginations, his tireless provocation of both us and the system and his total lack of fear. He was not afraid to instill fear either. He could be fierce and would stare at you for a long time without saying a word. You were transfixed. What was he thinking? What was he going to say next? You never quite knew. You were a little bit afraid. But you liked that.[6]

During this time, Pullman would teach during the day and write at least three pages of his novel at night. In his tiny shed at the back of the garden,

Pullman's now famous characters were born, including Lyra Belaqua and Will, Lord Asriel, and Mrs. Coulter.

In 1976, Pullman's first important novel, *Galatea*, was published. It is a story of magical realism filled with zombies, people with no blood, mutant werewolves, and ghosts, and where a man named Browning falls in love with a beautiful robot named Galatea. This book has recently been rediscovered by Pullman's fans, but there are no plans for the book to be republished.

After teaching middle school for twelve years, Pullman became a teacher at Westminster College. He taught students about writing, Victorian novels, and how words and pictures fit together.

During this time he was busy writing. With the success of Pullman's plays and the publishing of his novel, *Galatea*, he began to believe that he was finally on his way to fulfilling his dream of being a writer.

Chapter 5

Heroes and Villains

Philip Pullman has always been a fan of mysteries. When he was young, he loved to read the famous Sherlock Holmes mysteries by British author Sir Arthur Conan Doyle. He thought he should try his hand at writing this genre.[1]

Pullman's experiences as a teacher had taught him how to tell stories properly. Having his students perform plays he wrote also taught him the craft of writing a scene. Pullman used these skills to write his first book for children.

"Count Karlstein" began as a play. Writing and performing this play was the most fun Pullman ever had, he said. This play has all the ingredients that young people love. There are ghosts, humor, and special effects. Published as a book in 1998, it was named as a New York Public Library Best

Book of the Year. The plot revolves around Count Karlstein, who lives in Switzerland in 1816. The evil Count Karlstein plots to abandon his two nieces in a hunting lodge as prey for the Demon Huntsman and his ghostly hounds. Following Pullman's theme of strong female characters, the evil count is outwitted by Lucy, Charlotte, and the maid Hildi.

In the Sally Lockhart mystery quartet, Pullman says he found his "voice" as a children's writer.[2] He discovered Sally when he worked in a library in London. In a nearby antique shop where he was browsing one day, he came across several Victorian postcards. In one of the pictures a little girl sits on the lap of a man, both looking sad because the mother has died. In the second postcard, the mother is seen looking down from heaven, dressed like an angel. These cards remained on Pullman's desk for years and one day he found himself thinking about the people in the pictures. Slowly a story began to take shape and the characters began to come alive.

In his imagination, the characters talked to him and told him their names. Pullman also saw a teenage girl who was in terrible trouble in the background of the pictures. From these events, Sally Lockhart was born. Pullman's stories often begin this way, with a picture that forms in his mind or one he sees as part of his daily life. These pictures and scenes begin to "speak" to him and beg to be brought to life by his masterful gift of storytelling.[3]

Sally Lockhart is a sixteen-year-old detective whose father has recently died under strange and mysterious circumstances. Sally lives in Victorian England in the 1890s. Pullman calls these books "historical thrillers, old-fashioned Victorian blood and guts thunder." His descriptions of this era are well researched and accurate.[4]

The Ruby in the Smoke, the first book in the mystery series, also began as a play. Philip liked the characters so much that he turned the play into a book. The main character, Sally Lockhart, is a sixteen-year-old orphan when the story begins. Soon, she finds herself in serious danger. She knows this has to do with the death of her father. In her investigation into his death she also discovers the deadly secret of the ruby in the smoke.

In the second book, *The Shadow in the North*, Sally is twenty-two years old. Setting out to right some wrongs, she challenges a wealthy man who runs an evil business called North Star. She uncovers a plot so horrific that it could eventually bring down the whole civilized world. Sally also develops a romantic relationship with her friend Frederick. Readers enjoy the characters, fast-paced writing, and engaging plot in this novel.

The third installment, *The Tiger in the Well*, finds Sally fighting for the rights of the poor and underprivileged. Sally is now the mother of a two-year-old daughter named Harriet. Sally sets out to help Jewish immigrants who are being swindled by an evil man who will stop at nothing to exploit them. The young girl who disappears at the end of

The Ruby in the Smoke appears again with difficulties that need to be worked out. Pullman plans to write more books in this series. He thinks Sally's daughter Harriet might be a main character in the next book.

Pullman's other works are not well known to American fans. Some of these are contemporary novels, *The Broken Bridge* and *The Butterfly Tattoo*. *The Broken Bridge* is semi-autobiographical. Pullman says he was writing about his own teenage years in north Wales, his discovery of the visual arts, and his love for this part of the world. The main character is Ginny Howard, who is fifteen and lives with her father, who is a widower, in northern Wales. Ginny's mother was from Haiti and was half African. She learns she has a half-brother and that her mother may still be alive. The book is full of suspense and drama and will keep readers engaged. The theme of strong female characters discovering their own world is apparent in this novel.

The Butterfly Tattoo was originally titled *The White Mercedes*. The publisher thought girls might not want to read a book about cars, so the title was changed, much to Pullman's dismay. This novel is a modern story in which the characters encounter both love and death. Seventeen-year-old Chris lives and works in Oxford, England, and falls in love with an elusive girl who is searching for her mother. It is a book about the heartbreaking results of placing trust in the wrong person.

Pullman's books cover a wide range of characters

and plot. *Thunderbolt Waxworks* is proof of his ability to write many and varied types of stories. This book features a group of boys in South London in 1894. They call themselves the "New Cut Gang." They are vagabonds who set out to solve a mystery involving counterfeit coins. There is a lot of action and humor, and once again the young people solve the problems through their own cleverness and ingenuity. Thunderbolt Dobney is the main character and leader of the gang. He grows as a person as he solves this mystery.

The Gas Fitters Ball continues the saga of the New Cut Gang. In this novel, full of gangsters, bookies, pickpockets, and thieves, the gang is relentlessly pursued by a murderer and no one knows when or where he might strike.[5]

Another of Pullman's successful school plays from his teaching days that has been published as a novel is *The Firework-Maker's Daughter.* Pullman wanted to use special effects at the school, including an elephant and fireworks. The play and book grew from those unusual ideas. Philip had to find a plot that would connect the elephant and the fire-fiend, the villain in this play. As time passed and the play progressed, he realized he was telling a story about the making of art. Lila is the main character and the firework-maker's daughter (another strong female character). More than anything, she wants to be a firework-maker too, but is prohibited because she is female. Lila's father wants her to marry and have a normal life. Lila, not one to be defeated, sets out to change her world. She faces her obstacles and overcomes the people and circumstances that would deny her dream. She must confront the evil fire-fiend, Razvani, and bring back the royal sulfur, a necessary ingredient for fireworks. This book was a Booklist Editor's Choice Award. It also received great reviews when it was performed as a play at the Lyric Theater in Hammersmith, England. The play also toured throughout England in 2005.[6]

As someone who loves ghost stories, Pullman thought he should write a very spooky play that would appeal to young readers' fears. His idea came to him while viewing an old clock in the Science Museum in London. He decided to devise a hair-raising, heart-pounding book about a clock. *Clockwork*, or *All Wound Up*, is the story of a murderous wind-up clock and a young prince who has a mechanical heart. Pacts with the devil and the evil Dr. Kalmenius add sinister elements to the story. The villains receive their well-deserved comeuppance in this ghostly tale. Pullman's theme of belief in the power of choice is central in this story. The characters follow their own paths and desires and reap the consequences of their actions. *Clockwork* is a very popular book and has been performed as a play all over England.

Philip Pullman is not one who shies away from unusual subjects for his books. *I Was a Rat* is an unusual title and a popular book whose main character is one of the rats from Cinderella. This rat was the one who was changed into a pageboy. The plot includes a kidnapping, a secret, very evil characters, and of course, a princess who comes to the rescue. The subtle themes are those of greed, hope, abuse of power, and the miracle of love. Pullman's positive themes are always ones of morality and looking for the best in people no matter who they are.

Pullman has also rewritten popular fairy tales and given them a twist to liven them up. One of these tales is *Spring-heeled Jack*, a graphic novel that portrays Philip's love of superheroes and comics. Other familiar rewritten stories are *Puss 'N Boots*, *Mosseycoat* (another variation of the Cinderella fairytale), and *Aladdin and the Enchanted Lamp*. All of these are tales Pullman enjoyed as a child and will be performed as a play in Bristol, England, during the 2005 and 2006 Christmas season.[7]

Pullman's books have something for every reader. His recurring themes of good vs. evil and young people working out their own problems through ingenuity are found in all of Pullman's books and readers will not be disappointed with them. Above all, his commitment to be true to the story is what makes his work powerful and compelling. His most important work was still to be written and these earlier books helped him perfect his skills for the big project that made him a superstar writer.

CHAPTER 6

THE BOOKS

Pullman's books are many and varied, but all contain the same themes of young people overcoming bad situations on their own. His main characters try to learn how to live and be good people by changing their world and making the best of the here and now, because that is where the joy of life is to be found. Pullman believes children can be and are courageous in their actions. Those are the young people he loves to write about.

Pullman's first adult book of some acclaim was the novel *Galatea* (Dutton) published in 1979. Mark Browning, a talented flute player, is the main character. He must go on a search to locate his wife, who is missing. Pullman's love of fantasy is revealed in the characters, some of whom are zombies, mutants, ghosts, and robotic creatures.

While on his quest, Browning falls madly in love with a beautiful robot named Galatea.[1]

Count Karlstein (Chatto & Windus) was one of Pullman's first published plays. The play was published as a book in 1982. Set in Switzerland in 1816, it is a terrifying story about an evil Demon Huntsman. One of the main characters is a young girl named Hildi, who tells the tale of evil to her younger brother Peter. Hildi is the teenage maid-servant who lives in Count Karlstein's castle. She hears that the evil count is planning to offer his two young nieces to Zamil the Demon Huntsman on Halloween Eve as part of an old bargain the two have made. Hildi and her brother, with the help of a teacher, plan to foil this exchange. It is a true horror story but balanced with humor.[2]

In 1982, Pullman's humorous novel *How To Be Cool* (Heinemann) was published. This novel is set in contemporary Britain and tells the story of a teenage boy who invents a device to measure how "cool" someone is. This book was adapted for television in Great Britain.

Pullman's first attempt at a series begins with the book *The Ruby in the Smoke* (Oxford University Press) published in 1987. The novel is set in Victorian England and features Sally Lockhart's quest to discover who killed her father and why. She also must learn the meaning of "the seven blessings" and who has the rare stolen ruby. This novel is a fast-paced thriller.[3]

The Shadow in the North (Oxford University Press), published in 1987, is the second in the

Most of Philip Pullman's books contain themes that involve young people overcoming adversity on their own.

series of Sally Lockhart mysteries and begins six years after *The Ruby in the Smoke*. Readers find twenty-two-year-old Sally, with her own consulting business. Her close friend Fred Garland is a photographer who also has his own private detective agency. He usually ends up enlisting Sally's help in his most mysterious cases. This novel involves a client who has lost a large sum of money. Sally is led from the slums of London to the corporate offices of the richest man in Europe. This novel is a page-turning thriller.[4]

The third installment in the Lockhart series is *The Tiger in the Well* (Viking, London) and was published in 1990. Sally is now the mother of a toddler. Her friend and father of her child, Fred Garland, has died. This mystery is about Sally and her struggle against a net of enemies that closes around her. It is a story for older readers and involves more mature themes.

Sixteen-year-old Ginny is the protagonist in Pullman's novel *The Broken Bridge* (Macmillan, London). It was published in 1990 and introduces readers to another strong female character. Ginny has always felt a close bond with her mother even though she has been raised by her father. Her mother is a talented painter from Haiti. Ginny is also a passionate artist. She is the only mixed-race person in her small Welsh village and this fact has caused her difficulties in her life. She discovers startling facts about her family that are shocking and turn her already troubled world upside down.[5]

Pullman's novel *The White Mercedes* (Macmillan) begins with the line, "Chris Marshall met the girl he was going to kill on a warm night in early June." A chance meeting with Jenny at an Oxford party leaves seventeen-year-old Chris with hopes of a summer romance, but no idea of the impending trouble. Chris is busy with his first summer job, but soon falls in love with Jenny. Her cheerful demeanor hides the dark uncertainty of her past. Chris misses all of the danger signs and before he knows it, he is caught in the sinister web of a criminal whose desire for revenge crushes all who stand in his way. Pullman fans will love the mystery and the complex characters. This book was also published under the title *The Butterfly Tattoo*. Publishers feared that males would not buy or want to read a book with the word butterfly in the title.

The Tin Princess (Knopf) is the fourth book in the Sally Lockhart series. Published in 1994, it begins as a realistic story, but there are times when readers might think it is a fantasy. It is set in Prague, where readers meet Carmen Ruiz, the crazy wife of Prince Rudolph's older crazy brother. Carmen is a strong character who must endure a murderous assault.

Mrs. Holland's maid, Adelaide, had vanished at the end of *The Tiger in the Well*. The novel picks up the story ten years later, in 1882. Jim Taylor has tracked Adelaide down. She has been secretly married to Prince Rudolph of Razkavia. The old king dies and Rudolph is crowned king. He is assassinated and Adelaide becomes queen. She has many enemies who try to harm her. This book is quite different from the previous three books in the series. It is a complex story of romance, intrigue, and adventure.

The Firework-Maker's Daughter (Scholastic) was originally approved as a play, written by Pullman when he was a teacher. Scholastic published the book in 1995. The play has been performed at the prestigious Oxford Playhouse in England.[6] This unique story is set "a thousand miles ago" and very far away. Lila, the young character, has grown up among her father's clutter and creations in his fireworks studio in China. Lila wants to follow in his footsteps and become a firework-maker. Her father, Lalchand, thinks more about finding a suitable husband for her.

Lila sets out to change her father's mind with the help of a friend, Chulak, keeper of the king's talking white elephant Hamlet. Lila is determined to discover what she must do to accomplish her goal to become a master firework-maker. She discovers the last thing she must have is the royal sulfur, which can only be found in the grotto of Razvani, the evil fire-fiend. Not a person to be deterred by obstacles, Lila is determined to achieve her goals.[7]

Clockwork, released in 1998, is one of Pullman's best short stories. The setting is the same as *Count Karlstein*, mid-nineteenth-century Europe. This is a spooky gothic tale told in the German fairy-tale tradition. Fritz, the village storyteller, discovers that Karl, the village clockmaker, has not been able to fulfill his job of making a new figure for the great town clock. Karl is the first to fail at this task. Karl decides to make a "bargain" with the evil character who will solve his problem. Young readers will enjoy the dark and mysterious tale.[8]

In 1999, a twisted fairy-tale-like story was published. This unique story introduces an unusual young boy named Roger, who shows up on the doorstep of a kindly shoemaker named Bob and his equally kind wife, Joan. The couple cleans up the boy and together they teach him proper hygiene and manners, and do their best to provide for the boy. In spite of Bob and Joan's kindness, Roger still has some problems. He is expelled from school and decides to run away and work in a traveling freak show. He soon falls in with a band of young burglars and ends up in prison, condemned to death. The inmates call him the monster of the sewers. In spite of the gloomy tone, the book is a hilarious spin-off of the well-known *Cinderella* story.[9]

Spring-Heeled Jack was first published in 1991 and has been reissued after Pullman's great success with *His Dark Materials* trilogy. This tale is set in Victorian London and is full of dark deeds and courage. This book is geared toward younger readers and introduces orphans Rod, Lily, and Ned, who are trying to hop on board a ship destined for the United States where they plan to begin a new life. The trio of youngsters soon meet up with the villainous Mack the Knife and his evil gang. The orphans are also being pursued by the directors of the orphanage from which they escape. The children find supporters for their cause as well. A good-hearted sailor, a small stray dog, and the hero, Spring-Heeled Jack, a caped figure in tights, top hat, and magic shoes, save the day. This book is an adventure story full of humor and Pullman's quirky but lovable characters.[10]

Pullman has also tried his hand at retelling a classic tale, *Puss 'N Boots*. This quaint story is expanded with spooky new characters and unusual plot twists. Puss is still the crafty and scheming feline who convinces the king and princess that his poverty stricken master, Jacques, is really royalty. When the princess is kidnapped by the evil ogre's henchman, Jacque and Puss concoct a scheme to rescue her and are helped by eerie ghouls and a hermit.

Pullman is a huge fan of the British detective character Sherlock Holmes. He adapted his favorite Holmes story, *Sherlock Holmes and the Limehouse Mystery*, as a play. The sleuth Holmes and his faithful companion, Watson, solve a mystery when a young lady enlists the pair's help. Her beloved uncle has returned from a trip to the Far East with an odd-looking whip. This story combines drama and humor with adventure in classic Pullman style.

Pullman's readers demanded to know and read more about Lyra, the main character in the *His Dark Materials* trilogy. *Lyra's Oxford* (Knopf) is a companion book and continues Lyra Belaqua's story and adventures at school. The book is beautiful, bound in red cloth, and contains maps of Oxford.

Pullman's latest novel, *The Scarecrow and the Servant* (Knopf, 2005), tells the tale of Mr. Pandolfo and his homemade scarecrow, who comes to life when struck by lightning. Jack meets up with Scarecrow and together they have many adventures involving soldiers and crooks. Pullman's masterful storytelling provides humor and colorful characters.[11]

CHAPTER 7

DAEMON'S DARKNESS AND DUST

Fans of Philip Pullman know his books are not like any other fantasy books. There is always something unique that sets them apart. It is Pullman's gift. The worlds that he creates are often realistic, with a twist of the fantastic. Lyra's world is set in Victorian England and yet is still in the present day. One wonderful part of Lyra's world is daemons. Everyone in this world has a daemon.

A daemon is a person's wonderful, inseparable life companion. A daemon is a creature of a person's very essence, a person's being, or soul. Your daemon is always with you, so you are never alone. A daemon is a person's guide, conscience, and protector. At times a daemon seems to be telepathic. A daemon also has the ability to reason and provide love to its human.[1]

Children's daemons can change shapes depending on the emotional demands of their human or the situation. Lyra's own daemon is a cat, Pantalaimon, meaning "all merciful" in Greek. Pan, as Lyra affectionately calls him, changes into a fluttering moth to warn her of danger, as he does when she is walking down the darkening hall in the very first paragraph of *The Golden Compass*. He also becomes an ermine when he wraps himself around Lyra's neck to warm her.[2]

Children's daemons change, but when adolescence sets in, a daemon begins a process called "settling." At this time, the daemon will become one creature and maintain that shape until death. The emotions of adults are also revealed through their daemons. Mrs. Coulter's seemingly innocent questions to Lyra are betrayed by her daemon, a golden monkey, whose fur stands on end, demonstrating Mrs. Coulter's evil thoughts and intentions.

Daemons provide a way for the character to have a dialogue as they consider and work out problems they have to solve. Pullman treats daemons like human characters. We learn about their physical traits as well as their character traits from the stories. We know what they are thinking.

Daemons have conflicts with other daemons as well, which gives them a realistic personality. When Mrs. Coulter's daemon, the golden monkey, attacks Pan, Lyra feels the pain as if she herself is being attacked. Daemons also have conflicts with their human. At times they can sense future danger

Pullman's illustration of Lyra, taken from *Northern Lights*. On his website, Pullman wrote that this was the "hardest drawing of all," and that "because she's leaving her world . . . there's no border around this picture. The boundaries are all dissolved."

the child may not see and can act almost like a parent.

A daemon cannot stray far from its human. If they are separated by more than a few feet terrible physical and emotional trauma causes pain for both. Pullman refers to this experience as "pulling."[3]

Separation from one's daemon causes an emotional death in the human. Roger, Lyra's orphaned friend from the clay pits, becomes cold and emotionally crippled when his daemon is severed from him by the evil Oblation Board.

People cannot change their daemons. The daemon will "settle" into a form that will mirror the human's personality. Daemons are almost always the opposite sex of their human. They fill a void in their humans and are a perfect complement.[4]

Young readers often wonder what their own daemon might be. While people cannot choose their own daemons, Pullman suggests readers should ask several of their friends to write down the type of animal they remind them of. He also recommends that this activity should be done anonymously.

Pullman's fans are also curious about what his own daemon might be. He has given this question a lot of thought, since he is asked it over and over. Pullman believes his own daemon might be a creative bird, such as a jackdaw or a magpie, a bird that is attracted to shiny, glittering objects. He explains it this way: "A magpie is a thief. It takes things that belong to someone else, bright and

shiny things and makes them his own. And that's
what writers do, isn't it?"[5]

Daemons are just one element Pullman utilizes
to invite his readers into his stories. Another mys-
tical element Pullman has created for his trilogy is
"Dust." Dust is the whole reason for the horrible
experiments at the Bolvanger Experimental
Station. It is what the Church wants to destroy
and this is the task Mrs. Coulter and Lord Asriel
have been given as representatives of this Church.
Dust is to be feared, and if it can be controlled the
Church believes that "original sin" will be eliminated
forever. When a child and its daemon are separated
by the process of "intercission," dust will no
longer have any effect on the child. The child will
no longer have an awareness of human sexuality
and of the many problems that accompany this
human need and desire. Dust is the cause.[6]

The complete definition of Dust provides a better understanding of its complexities: "Dust is the
physical manifestation of conscious thought and
love."[7] Dust is flowing away through the windows
created by the subtle knife, until Will and Lyra fall
in love, creating enough Dust to halt the flow for
a time. The angels (who are made of Dust) close
the remaining windows, and ask Will to destroy
the subtle knife in order to protect Dust.

Pullman's idea of Dust came to him early on in
the writing of the trilogy:

> This notion of dark matter—something all-pervasive
> and absolutely necessary but totally mysterious in
> the universe—was one of the starting points for the
> story. It is a wonderful gift for a storyteller, because

Pullman's illustration of the subtle knife.

if nobody knows what it is, you can make it be what you'd like! Quite early on, too, I found the phrase from *Paradise Lost* which gives me the title for the whole trilogy: "Unless the almighty make them ordain/ His dark materials to create more worlds." That seemed to fit exactly the kind of thing I was talking about, so I leapt on it. And the idea that Dust should be in some sense symbolic of consciousness and original sin—what the churches traditionally used to understand as sin, namely disobedience, the thing that made us human in the first place—seemed too tempting to ignore, so I put them together.[8]

Pullman also uses the Bible as a reference point for the term Dust. God curses Adam after eating the Forbidden fruit, and states, "For dust thou art and unto dust shalt thou return."

Pullman also believes there are various meanings for Dust. It can be original sin, the form of thoughts not yet spoken, dark matter (thus the title of the trilogy, *His Dark Materials*), or particles of consciousness. Dust in and of itself has no power to shape human lives. Only personal responsibility and choices made by people can do that. Dust is also the force that allows the alethiometer (*The Golden Compass*) to work. It flows around the Aurora Borealis (the Northern Lights), works its way through parallel universes, and adheres to adult humans. The alethiometer was a gift given to Lyra by the Master of Jordan College. It is a truth teller and Lyra must teach herself how to use it.

Mrs. Coulter even tries to put a positive spin on the intercission experiments as she talks to Lyra. Mrs. Coulter tells Lyra, "All that happens is a little cut and then everything is peaceful. Forever! You see, your daemon's a wonderful friend and companion when you're young, but at the age we call puberty . . . daemons bring all sorts of troublesome thoughts and feelings, and that's what lets Dust in."[9]

Lyra's maturity and Pan's guidance throughout *The Golden Compass* allow her to question all she has been told about Dust. Pantalaimon tells Lyra, "We've heard them all talk about Dust, and they're so afraid of it, and you know what? We believed them, even though we could see that what they were doing was wicked and evil and wrong . . . we thought Dust must be bad too, because they said so. But what if it isn't?"[10] This realization helps drive Lyra on a quest to the North and to other worlds.

Parallel worlds are an important element in *His Dark Materials*. Will Parry is a character readers meet in the second book, *The Subtle Knife*. Will lives in our world. Lyra and Will's worlds are similar in many ways and yet very different in others. Parallel worlds allow Pullman to broaden the story and to keep readers engaged with his gift of descriptive detail. Pullman's worlds have their own different histories and cultures. Lyra's world is human and set in late Victorian England. Will Parry is from a world like ours, a world where people have daemons but they do not have the capacity to see them. They do not even know they exist until taught to discover them much later in the series.

Will Parry stumbles into a world called Cit`agazze, a Mediterranean type of city full of deadly specters and evils, when he falls through a window at Oxford University. Another world Pullman creates is the world of the Mulefa. These unique creatures travel on seed pods created by giant trees that grow in their world.

The Mulefas are very conscious of the environment and are compassionate stewards of their world. The Harpies are the guardians of another world, the Land of the Dead. Harpies torment the dead spirits and it is in this world where Lyra discovers the only way to live is through following truth.

The connection between worlds is an important element that helps tie the story together. Pullman explains his use of parallel worlds and the fact that it is possible they may exist through studies he has made of scientific writings about quantum mechanics and string theory. Fans of Pullman's trilogy know that the multiple worlds help to make these stories fascinating.

CHAPTER 8

CONTROVERSY AND CRITICS

*P*hilip Pullman and his *His Dark Materials* trilogy have come under much criticism for "killing God" in the third book, *The Amber Spyglass*, and for trying to promote his idea of the republic of Heaven on Earth. As a result, Pullman has been accused of proclaiming an "anti-Christian" message in his books. The *Catholic Herald* in Britain has stated that Pullman's books, *The Golden Compass*, *The Subtle Knife,* and *The Amber Spyglass* are "truly the stuff of nightmares and are worthy of the bonfire."[1] Some of Pullman's books have been condemned as profane and have been banned in some places. Pullman has even been called "the most dangerous author in Britain."[2]

Outstanding sales of Pullman's book in the United States are a worry to many Christian religious groups. Some groups are warning parents to keep the books out of the hands of their children and have called the books "satanic, dark and terrifying."[3] British journalist Peter Hitchens believes Pullman has a sinister agenda and knows perfectly well what he is doing when he writes books proclaiming the death of God to young readers.[4]

Pullman is fascinated by the relationship between religion and science. He believes this is where the true meaning of our existence will be found. While Pullman will be the first to admit he does not do science, but fiction, he is fascinated by it and it is part of the philosophy that he conveys in his books.

Pullman believes the function and purpose of scientific research allows him to make up new facts that are convincing in his stories and also leads him to believe there is no scientific evidence that God exists.[5]

However, religion is an important part of Pullman's trilogy. The books are based on John Milton's seventeenth-century poem, *A Paradise Lost*. This is Milton's retelling of the story of the beginning of man according to the book of Genesis in the Bible.

In Pullman's trilogy, religion, represented by the Church, is evil, a negative and an oppressive thing. It is barbaric and cruel. In Lyra's world, the Church is Roman Catholic. The Pope is replaced by the Magisterium. These people are in constant battle to see who can be the most powerful in this world. Anyone who goes against the Church or who studies subjects without approval from the Magisterium is considered evil and killed.[6]

In *His Dark Materials* the people who represent the church are portrayed as evil and these are the people in power. The scientist, Mary Malone, is a former nun who left the Church to pursue the truth. She tells Lyra in *The Amber Spyglass* that the Christian religion "is a very powerful and convincing mistake."[7]

Lord Asriel, who is really Lyra's father, takes the role of Satan in the rebellion against God. The Authority, according to Pullman, was the first angel to morph out of Dust and declares to everyone that he is their creator. In *The Amber Spyglass*, the Authority (God) is seen as ancient, senile, weary, and without his senses.[8] He has given most of his power to the angel Metatron. These are the parts of the books that are so upsetting to readers of faith and have brought criticism of Pullman from religious leaders and others.

Pullman's critics believe that he is trying to promote his own personal view of religion and faith. Pullman believes that God may exist and does not want to persuade anyone to give up their faith. He states he just has not seen any scientific evidence that God exists.[9]

Pullman believes that organized religion is part of what is wrong with the world. He cites the Crusades in the Holylands and the Salem Witch Trials in colonial America when Puritan believers executed people they thought were possessed by evil. His dislike of organized religion does not

Pullman displays his book, *The Amber Spyglass*, at the
Whitbread Book Awards on January 22, 2002.

come from a disbelief in the Bible or in God, but from the way people have used the name of God to have and hold power over others. Pullman states:

> My dislike of religion comes from history. It comes from records of the Inquisition, persecuting heretics (those opposed to church beliefs) and torturing Jews, and it comes from the other side too, from the Protestants burning the Catholics. It comes from the pursuit of innocent and crazy old women and from the Puritans burning and hanging the witches—it comes not only from the Christian church, but also from the Taliban. Every single religion with a monotheistic God (one God) ends up persecuting other people.[10]

"My dislike of religion comes from history."

—Philip Pullman

Ironically, some of Pullman's fondest childhood memories are of going to the church as a young boy, where his grandfather was a minister. He enjoyed reading the Bible and singing the beautiful hymns. However, Pullman believes people can have good values and morals without any belief in God.

One Christian website, "Facing the Challenge," claims Pullman is trying to say that we all just need to be nice to each other, but that he leaves God out of the equation. Pullman responds: "If there is no God, then no one needs to question why? If there is no God, no judgement, no after-life, why should a person care whether I hurt, damage or destroy other people? My point is that if there is no God, there is no reason for me to try to make earth like heaven."[11]

Critics have stated that Pullman's views and philosophy are in his books. Pullman explains that his portrayal of the Authority in his books repre-sents the corruption of the church. Pullman believes that if all people, no matter what their beliefs, try to uphold the values of all religions while doing away with evil by their own actions, there can be a republic of heaven here on Earth. In such a case, no one would have to believe the Christian myth of life after death in heaven.[12]

Pullman's view on religion is not the only rea-son he has been criticized. He has also come under fire by fans and devotees of the popular and beloved British author C. S. Lewis, a giant in chil-dren's literature, especially in Great Britain and Europe. Most young people have heard of his seven book series *The Chronicles of Narnia*, and have read at least one of them. The series includes *The Magician's Nephew*; *The Lion, the Witch and the Wardrobe*; *The Horse and his Boy*; *Prince Caspian*; *The Voyage of the Dawn Treader*; *The Silver Chair*; and *The Last Battle*. Lewis wrote these books from 1950–1956 and introduced magical worlds and characters to his readers. Centaurs, witches, and other odd creatures share the world of Narnia with regular human beings and are therefore compared to Pullman's trilogy which has some similarities with Lewis's work.

C. S. Lewis was born in England in 1898 and died in 1963. Lewis's Christian-based books are found in millions of homes around the world and convey a moral message that can stay with the reader for a lifetime.

Pullman first read *The Chronicles of Narnia* when he was a teacher and has criticized the books and their author at every opportunity. Pullman describes the books as being "anti-life, cruel and so unjust." Pullman believes the *Narnia* books are racist, anti-women, and full of Lewis's Christian propaganda.[13]

Pullman supports his criticism of the books with examples from some of the books in the series. Pullman explains that in the book *The Last Battle*, a character named Susan is sent to hell for growing up. The young girl becomes interested in boys, clothes, and lipstick. All of these are natural longings for a young girl. These are events that Pullman believes should be celebrated as a natural passage and not looked upon as something evil and sinister. Pullman also believes that C. S. Lewis did not like women in general or sexuality at all, at least not when he wrote the *Narnia* books.

Mark and Carol Ryan, authors of *Killing God: The Propaganda of His Dark Materials*, written for the Christian Research Institute, believe Pullman misrepresents part of the Lewis books. They insist Lewis was saying that Susan's problem was not growing up, but that she decided to leave the stories of *Narnia* behind. Susan does not go to hell, she is just not in the train accident that kills her siblings and her parents and sends them to heaven.

Pullman also criticizes Lewis's ending of the series. Lewis allows the children and their parents to be killed in a train wreck which tries to convey the message to young readers that the family is now better off dead. This is because in the Christian faith when someone dies they go to heaven to live with God and this is their reward for believing when they were alive. Pullman thinks this is a cruel trick Lewis plays on his readers. All the while he is trying to push the Christian faith on his readers.

Pullman believes that joy must be found on earth while we live. He argues for what he calls "a republic of heaven" where people live their lives as richly and fully as they can because there is no life beyond. The republic of heaven is one where people make moral choices and are kind to others and to the environment.[14]

Pullman's critics accuse him of trying to preach and spread his gospel of the republic of heaven, which states that humans are in charge of their own fate and the joy and rewards are only to be found as we live out our lives on earth. When asked to explain the difference between the "kingdom" of heaven and the "republic" of heaven Pullman said, "This world where we live is our home. Our home is not elsewhere. There is no elsewhere. This is a physical universe where physical beings are made of material stuff. This is where we live."[15]

Pullman is not concerned about his critics and believes all of the fuss and controversy surrounding his books have increased sales for him and have placed the books into the hands of people who might not have heard about them otherwise. For him it is a win-win situation.

Pullman knows that stories pass down moral values from one generation to the next. They teach about the people and the world humans have made. He confirms this belief stating, "We don't need a list of rights and wrongs, tables of do's and don'ts: we need books, time and silence. 'Thou shalt not' is soon forgotten, but once upon a time lasts forever."[16]

Chapter 9

Success and Storytelling

Like great British authors before him, such as Lewis Carroll, C.S. Lewis, and J. R. R. Tolkien, who were also alumni of Oxford University, Philip Pullman's books appear to have real lasting qualities and are quite possibly destined to become classics. Influenced indirectly by these authors, Pullman has taken his readers down holes, through wardrobes, and into imaginary worlds where his characters fight the big battles of good vs. evil through their own ingenuity and intuition. These characters learn, as we all do, by making mistakes and by growing as individuals through their choices.

While very pleased with the success of all of his books, Pullman is still very excited over the success that *His Dark Materials* trilogy has seen as a stage production. The play first opened in December 2003 to sellout crowds at the Olivier Theatre, which is part of the National Theatre in London.

"It was a wonderful experience working with people like Nicholas Hytner, the Director of the National Theatre, and Nicholas Wright, the man who adapted the books for the stage production. The adaptation is superb," said Pullman.[1] The play's second run finished in March of 2005.

Pullman is the first to admit, "it was a difficult task to turn the books into a play. There are key characters that had to be omitted and the story had to be shortened, but it is brilliant, it is perfect."[2] Pullman anxiously awaited the first-night opening production of the novels. He states:

> The first night [of *His Dark Materials*] was actually an anti-climax, because they had come up against some big technical problems they hadn't expected. The production used all the facilities of the most complex stage in Britain, and with only a week to get the whole complicated story into the theatre after eighteen months of workshop and rehearsal, there were bound to be some things that didn't work. So my wife and I drove to London and parked the car and went into the theatre to get our tickets, and found ourselves surrounded by a throng of disappointed people who were being told that the performance couldn't take place, and that they'd have to come back another time. Oh, and could I go and sign books in the theatre bookshop? So I did that to keep the customers happy while my wife spent a jolly evening drinking wine in the Green Room with the actors. But when the play finally did open, it worked sensationally well. I wish I could say

that it was a huge thrill and I just sat there trembling with excitement as tears of happiness ran down my cheeks—but in fact I just watched it with critical attention, thinking "That works" and "That doesn't work" and "Maybe we should cut this" and "He's putting the wrong emphasis on that word" and "She should stand still and not wriggle about" and "He does that shy half-smile very well " and "The music is good here" and "The bears are moving too much" and "The witches look good" and "I can't hear what he's saying" and "The daemons are brilliant" and "He's got too many props to deal with" and so on, and so on, and so on. But it was a truly wonderful experience working with people (the playwright Nicholas Wright, the director Nicholas Hytner, the actors, all of whom were splendid, but Anna Maxwell Martin and Dominic Cooper were outstanding) who were just so talented, so quick to understand, so sympathetic to the story. And to see a full house night after night, and to think of the box office receipts, was fun too."[3]

The Olivier Theatre, part of the National Theatre in London, is the perfect location for the play because of the type of stage there, called a drum-revolve. The stage can revolve during a performance so that all audience members may see the many scenes being performed.

One of the greatest challenges of the play was how to create the daemons. In a parallel universe where the first book begins, everyone has a visible daemon, an animal that embodies the soul of the character. Giles Cadle, the set designer, believed that puppets would be the answer to the daemon dilemma. Jeff Curry designed the daemon puppets (he also worked with Julie Taymor, of "Lion King"

Philip Pullman stands alongside actress Joan Collins after the British Book Awards at London's Grosvenor House Hotel on March 5, 2002.

fame). He decided the effect of the daemon would be best produced by having the faces and bodies be almost see-through so they would have a light and airy appearance. He wanted them to look as if they came from the spirit world.

Costume designer Jon Morrell created more than two hundred and fifty costumes for the play for more than eighty characters. Scene changes occurred nearly every three minutes with fifty-five different locations being depicted in each of the two plays. Fans will be thrilled to know that a movie is in the works, but no date has been set for the release.[4]

Pullman no longer writes his stories in a shed at the back of the garden. His good fortune has recently allowed him to move to a larger house, a sixteenth century English farmhouse, just outside of Oxford, England, where he has lived for more than thirty years. His new writing place is a large, bright room lined with books. Pullman writes at a raised desk and then types his words into a computer. He loves to work with wood and takes breaks from his writing to work on a current project which might involve making something for his grandson. His study is home to a carpenter's vise, a band saw, and other woodworking tools.[5]

Pullman's decision to move to a larger and more private home meant leaving his potting shed where his beloved characters were written into life. He decided to give the shed to a fellow writer, Ted Dewan, who in turn has agreed to pass it on to another writer for use.[6]

Pullman's good fortune has also become both a blessing and a curse. He loves to write, but he is also in great demand as a speaker. This limits his writing time. His typical day begins around 7:30 A.M. when he takes his wife a cup of tea. He reads a newspaper (sometimes several) while he eats his breakfast. Pullman begins writing around 9:30 A.M. and works until lunchtime with an occasional break for coffee along the way. Usually, he tries to write three pages by then. If he meets his writing goals, he allows himself time in the afternoon to spend on his woodworking hobby. He loves to write and always writes with a ballpoint pen on narrow-lined paper. "The paper has to have a gray or blue margin and two holes." He writes on one side of the paper and when he gets to the bottom of the last page, he finishes the last sentence at the top of the next, so he never faces an empty page the following day. After a story is finished he will type it into his computer. He will read it all over again, "think it is horrible, and get very depressed!"[7]

After lunch Pullman watches "Neighbors," a British soap opera and then walks his two pugs, Hogarth and Nellie. He is a man who likes routines. "I have never been interested in traveling, really. It is uncomfortable, hot, full of foreigners. I don't like going away. I am an old misery. I like staying home."[8]

Home is where Pullman is likely to be. He is currently writing his companion novel to the trilogy titled *The Book of Dust*. A few familiar characters from *His Dark Materials* will be included, but it is not a sequel. It will be a book of short stories about characters like the witch Serafina Pekkala and the hot-air balloon captain Lee Scoresby. No publication date has been set, but Pullman fans will be looking forward to this book. Pullman has sold the movie rights for the trilogy to New Line Cinema. The BBC British television is interested in making a series based on Pullman's Sally Lockhart novels.

Pullman also is pursuing his artistic endeavors. He drew the small pictures that begin each chap-

"I don't like going away. . . . I like staying home."

—Philip Pullman

ter in the British version of *The Golden Compass*, titled *Northern Lights*. He also drew the pictures that begin each chapter of the British version of *The Subtle Knife*. Pullman hopes when these books are republished in the United States they will include his drawings. Each picture was drawn in ink and black watercolor on white Bristol boards. They are six centimeters square. Pullman had to learn not to put too much detail in, because the intricate details in the drawings disappear due to the small size of the print and the course paper that the books are printed on. So, the images are stronger and simpler.[9]

Pullman's zodiac wheel illustration. All the drawings
Pullman did for the *His Dark Materials* series were done
in ink and black watercolor.

Other interests that keep Pullman busy when not writing include his involvement in a local fight to save a boatyard on the Oxford Canal. It is in a part of the city named Jericho. People asked Pullman for his assistance because the characters in *The Golden Compass* known as gyptians worked in the clay pits by the boatyard. Pullman explains:

> There has been a boatyard on the site for over a hundred years, but the site itself belongs to a group called British Waterways. They sold it to a developer who wants to put up houses. The city council has refused permission for the project. I wanted to help because the boatyard is the only place for many miles around where narrow boats can be lifted out of the water for repairs and maintenance. They need to have this work done every four years or so in order to be certified as fit for use. There are also 120 people and their families who currently live on the water and they will have to sell their boats and find somewhere ashore, or move somewhere else just for the sake of a few new homes. It doesn't make sense to me. The boatyard is a good place.[10]

Another passionate interest of Pullman's is global warming. He has been watching the weather for a long time, in a casual way, but recently he purchased a weather station that is linked to his computer so he can track temperature, barometric pressure, humidity, and so on. Pullman believes that we do not experience hard winters anymore, that spring arrives earlier each year, and that insect pests are no longer killed off by frost. He also believes birds begin to nest sooner that they used to and that summers are unbearably hot. The evidence is overwhelming that human activity has played a part in causing these unusual phenomena. Pullman believes that those who deny it are either in the direct pay of the oil corporations or intent on serving some sort of political agenda. The evidence is just too great to ignore, he claims.[11]

His many interests and his strict discipline will ensure that Philip Pullman is writing and entertaining his readers for many years to come. He will use his life, his interests, his imagination, and the desire to tell the truth in his stories to keep Pullman readers on the edge, waiting for his next story.

IN HIS OWN WORDS

The following interview was conducted by the author with Philip Pullman via email in October 2004. The author would like to thank Mr. Pullman for taking the time out of his very busy schedule to answer all of her questions.

Who is Philip Pullman?

I don't really know. I don't think about him very much. He would like to be anonymous and invisible, but it's too late.

Rumor has it here in the U. S. that Philip Pullman wears only red shoelaces? True?

I also wear green ones. I like red shoelaces because . . . I think they look good!

When you were young you had the privilege of traveling with your family to many exotic places. How did these travels inspire or affect your writing?

I think they gave me a sense of how large and

varied the world is. When you travel by sea you have a much truer sense of the scale of things than when you fly.

Who are some people past or present that have inspired you in some way and are people whom you admire?

Artists, composers, poets, novelists, scientists—people like that. Beethoven, Vincent Van Gogh, William Blake, Jane Austen, Charles Darwin . . .

In another interview you have stated that "I write for the boy I once was." Who is the boy Philip?

He was elusive and introverted, on the fringe of things looking in, never at the center. He read a great deal.

Will you please tell the readers something about your family? Wife? Sons? Family interests?

My wife's name is Jude, and my two sons are Jamie and Tom. Jamie and his wife Anne are now the parents of two children, Freddie and Katherine. Tom is a Ph.D. student at Cambridge and Jamie is a professional viola player.

Do you receive a lot of fan mail?

The level of fan mail goes up and down according to whether a book of mine is in the best seller lists or not. I do get a fair amount from schools. I try to answer every letter, but I have to have a standard reply because otherwise I would be doing nothing else.

What is a hero to you? Are Lyra and Will heroes at the end of the trilogy? Why or why not? What people do you admire as heroes? Why?

I admire people with courage. Courage is almost the most important virtue. I don't know if Lyra and Will are heroes; that's for the reader to decide.

Can you please discuss the wonderful drawings that you created for each chapter in The Golden Compass*? (titled* Northern Lights *in Britain)*

I did a drawing for the chapter-heading of each chapter in the first two books. They are all significant in their different way. For example, the lantern projector at the beginning of Chapter 2 in *The Golden Compass* throws a beam of light directly at the first words where it is set into the text at the top left; and the picture of Lyra, with the final chapter, is the only one without a frame. Lyra looks directly out and up at the sky—the barriers have dissolved, there is nothing holding her in. The ones I like best are those that reproduce well, like the one of the ship with Chapter Two of *The Subtle Knife* and the skulls in their niches with Chapter Three of *The Golden Compass*.

This may seem like a strange question, but it is one I must ask. You seem to have a preference for the letter L when it comes to assigning names to your characters. Perhaps this is just a coincidence, but perhaps not? Is there any significance of the letter L? Examples, Lyra (His Dark Materials), Lila and her father, Lalchand (Firemaker's Daughter) and Lockhart (Sally Lockhart Series.) Any comment?

Coincidence! and you've forgotten Lee Scoresby. But my preference is for names that are euphonious, and L has a good sound as an initial letter.

What did you love the most about teaching? Do you ever miss this?

I enjoyed having an audience for the stories I used to tell. But I think I did it for long enough. I certainly don't miss all the downsides of teaching: the preparation, the marking, the continual struggle for discipline and order, the weariness of coping with idiotic bosses . . .

In your trilogy, His Dark Materials, how did you develop the concept of the Mulefa? What is their primary purpose in your books and whom do they represent?

I don't like interpreting my own work, but I suppose you could say that they represent a sort of benign way of interacting with the natural world while still having the sort of reflective and complex self-consciousness that characterizes humanity.

Did you write the trilogy to be "provocative" about your view of Christianity (organized religion) and its many failings or was there really a story that Philip Pullman needed to tell besides the obvious wonderful tales in the books?

I was just telling a story. Really—that's all.

The alethieometer is critical to the His Dark Material's trilogy, what are the origins of the symbols that are encased within the outer border?

Some of them are well-known emblems from the Renaissance tradition of symbolism, and some I just made up. But they all work in that symbolic way.

Why do you think young readers and perhaps people in general are so drawn to "dark forces"?

Because being wicked is more exciting than being good. In one of my contemporary novels, 'The Broken Bridge', two girls are discussing the boyfriend of one of them, Rhiannon, who says that unfortunately, Peter (that's his name) is too kind. Ginny is puzzled by this. Surely kindness is a good thing? But Rhiannon points out that kindness isn't sexy. What's more, she goes on, kind people would love to be sexy, though they never are; but sexy people don't care whether they're kind or not. So there you are: there's your answer. People would rather be sexy than kind.

You have stated that "stories are the most important thing in the world, Without stories we would not be human beings at all."

Why do you believe this is true?

Well, I believe it's true because every human society we know about has told stories, and because the best stories (those that have lasted the longest) are those that tell us what it's like to be a human being.

Where does the reader ``find'' Philip Pullman in his stories?

On the back flap.

You have the privilege of receiving so many honors for your writing. How has this changed you as a person and as a writer.

It's one more thing to struggle against. I was vain enough already. Now I'm in danger of becoming a monster of prodigious conceit.

Your trilogy is about strong friendship and loyalty and yet in the end there is a theme of betrayal? Does Lyra really betray Roger and Pan? And if so, why?

No, she doesn't. But it feels to her as if she does.

You also have the honor of being made a CBE, even Americans recognize this great honor. Can you describe the experience please.

I don't know who decides to offer these honours. You get a letter from the Prime Minister's office asking if you'd accept it, and you can refuse, if you don't want it. Anyway I said yes. You have to go to Buckingham Palace and the Queen hangs a medal around your neck along with a hundred or so other people who are getting honours that day. It's interesting, but it's all a bit absurd.

You have stated that your stories come to you as a series of unconnected pictures. Are these pictures in color? Do you think this is a gift you have? How do you weave them into a story?

It's like daydreaming. The pictures are in colour, but that's not a big thing; I'm not greatly interested in colour. Like William Blake, I prefer form. I sit and think about them until I see a way of connecting them together.

Does it bother you when you must, for the sake of the story, kill off one of your characters? It is very sad for your readers.

I'm gratified to have generated so many tears among my readers. If it's any consolation, it makes me cry to churn the stuff out. I dread writing the bits I know will have that effect, but it has to be done. I sit there sobbing like a baby as my trembling fingers move the pen through the lake of tears forming on the page. Incidentally, this is why I use a ballpoint. The Spotted Owl fountain pen would be little use to me in those passages. Then a little later I read it through, dry-eyed, and see if I can screw up the anguish a couple of notches to make it even more heart-wrenching. No, that's not true. I do cry. I also laugh immoderately at the jokes, which hardly anyone else has ever noticed. HDM is full of them. Like Mr. Pooter, I sometimes wake in the night thinking about them, and roars of hearty laughter shake the bed. But I do avoid the saddest bits when I'm reading it aloud, on a book tour, for example. Dignity must be preserved. I couldn't avoid them when I was doing the audiobook, though. The only way of getting through is to take it steadily and swallow a great deal.

Your illustrations in the first two books are wonderful, do you ever see Philip Pullman becoming a very serious artist? Do these scenes you paint come to your mind's eye the same way your stories do?

Yes, but you have to sketch them many times, just as you have to write over and over again till you get it right.

What are your very favorite scenes from the National Theatre production of His Dark Materials? Why?

The opening, which is magical; and the end, for the same reason; and the descent into the world of the dead, which is chilling and majestic.

Do you title your chapters before you write them or after and are these titles difficult to think of? What are some of your favorite titles?

Some of them come easily and some are very hard to find. My favourite is "The Idea Of North", which I stole from a famous radio programme made by the Canadian pianist Glenn Gould.

You have stated that you especially like the U. S. Knopf edition covers that have been painted by Eric Rohmann. What is it that you like about these paintings? They are very beautiful, but I did not picture any of the characters in my mind's eye to look like these renditions.

I like the atmosphere. There's a simplicity and beauty and magic about them which I've never seen anywhere else.

It is well known that you love the old comic book heroes, Batman, Superman, etc. What is it that you like about them? Is it the story, the presentation, both? Do you think readers today are still looking for superheroes?

I just like that way of telling a story. I first saw real comics when I was a boy in Australia in the 1950s. They had American comics there which we did not see at home in England. I just loved the excitement of Batman and Superman. I think people are looking for superheroes still, but we've become a bit cynical about them. They all have to have a flaw now before we can believe in them.

Can you update your American readers on the status of the film projection of His Dark Materials? Your new Book of Dust?

They're both still a long way off. I have begun to write [*The Book of Dust*] but I can't say anything about it.

Please finish this sentence: I am most passionate about:

Silence. If I were a judge, and someone came to my court and was found guilty of killing their neighbors because they played loud music all day and night, I would let them go with my blessing. There is too much noise in the world, and little of it is welcome.

CHRONOLOGY

1946—Philip Pullman is born in Norwich, England.

1948—Philip's brother, Francis, is born.

1953—Philip's father is killed when the plane he is flying for the Royal Air Force is shot down by terrorists.

1955—Philip's family moves to Australia after his mother remarries.

1956—Philip attends a prep school in Battersea, Australia.

1957—Philip's family moves back to Great Britain to live in North Wales.
Philip attends school with influential teacher Miss Enid Jones who introduces him to Milton's epic poem *Paradise Lost*.

1963—Philip enrolls at Exeter College at Oxford University, Oxford, England.

1968—Pullman graduates from Exeter College with a degree in English.

1969—Pullman wins his first writing award for a novel. He begins work with Moss Brothers clothiers.

1970—Pullman marries Judith Speller.

1971—Son Jamie is born.

1972–1986—Pullman teaches middle school students and finds his voice as a storyteller and writer of school plays.

1972—Pullman publishes his first novel, *The Haunted Storm*.

1976—Pullman's second novel, *Galatea*, is published.

1982—Son Tom is born.

1984—Pullman's play *Sherlock Holmes and the Adventure of the Sumatran Devil* is performed by the Polka Children's Theatre.

1985—*The Three Musketeers* play by Pullman is performed by the Polka Children's Theatre.

1985—First novel in the Sally Lockhart series, *The Ruby in the Smoke*, is published.

1986—Pullman becomes a part-time professor at Westminster College teaching students preparing to become teachers. The second novel in the Lockhart series, *The Shadow in the North*, is published.

1988—Pullman wins the United Kingdom Reading Award and the International Reading Association Children's Book Award.

1990—Pullman writes his play *Frankenstein*.

1991—*The Tiger in the Well* is published.

1993—Pullman begins an ambitious writing project based on *Paradise Lost*.

1994—*Thunderbolt's Waxwork* and *The Tin Princess* are published.

1995—*Northern Lights* (also known as *The Golden Compass*) is published.

1996—*Clockwork or All Wound Up* published. Pullman receives the Carnegie Medal, awarded to the writer of the most outstanding book for children in that year, and The Guardian's Children's Fiction Award for *The Golden Compass*.

1997—*The Subtle Knife*, the second book in the *His Dark Materials* trilogy, is published.

1998—Pullman receives the United Kingdom Reading Award.

2000—*The Amber Spyglass* is published, the last book in Pullman's *His Dark Materials* trilogy.

2002—Pullman is awarded the prestigious Whitbread Prize for *The Amber Spyglass*, the first time this prize has been awarded for a children's book. The American Library Association presents Pullman with the Arbuthnot Award for his contribution to children's literature. Pullman sells the movie rights for the *His*

Dark Materials trilogy to New Line Cinema.

2003—*Lyra's Oxford,* a companion book to the trilogy is published. Pullman's book *The Scarecrow and the Servant* is published to rave reviews.

2004—Pullman is honored as "The Greatest Briton in the Arts." He is awarded the CBE (Commander of the British Empire) by Queen Elizabeth.

2005—Pullman is awarded the prestigious Astrid Lindgren Award by the Swedish government.

Chapter Notes

Chapter 1. Servant of the Story

1. Nicholas Tucker, *Inside the World of Philip Pullman: Darkness Visible* (New York: iBooks, 2003), pp. 3–5.

2. "Author Pullman Made CBE at Palace," *BBC News*, March 10, 2004, <http://news.bbc.co.uk/1/he/entertainment/arts/3498840.stm> (September 26, 2005).

3. Christina Patterson, "Philip Pullman: Material Worlds," *The Independent*, November 12, 2004, <http://enjoyment.independent.co.uk/books/interviews/story.jsp?story=581889> (September 26, 2005).

4. Tucker, p. 92.

5. Patterson, "Philip Pullman: Material Worlds."

6. Philip Pullman, "I Have A Feeling This All Belongs To Me," n.d., <http://www.philip-pullman.com/pages/content/index.asp?PageID=84> (September 26, 2005).

7. Tucker, p. 23.

8. Ibid., p. 24.

9. Philip Pullman, "About the Writing," n.d., <http://www.philip-pullman.com.about_the_writing.asp> (December 9, 2004).

Chapter 2. Storytelling Seeds

1. Nicholas Tucker, *Inside the World of Philip Pullman: Darkness Visible* (New York: iBooks, 2003), p. 3.
2. Philip Pullman, "I Have A Feeling This All Belongs To Me," n.d., <http://www.philip-pullman.com/pages/content/index.asp?PageID=84> (September 26, 2005).
3. Philip Pullman, "Author Interview," *KidsReads.com*, September 9, 2004, <http://www.kidsreads.com/auathors/au-pullman-philip.asp/>
4. Tucker, p. 9.

Chapter 3. Comic Books and Superheroes

1. Philip Pullman, "I Have A Feeling This All Belongs To Me," n.d., <http://www.philip-pullman.com/pages/content/index.asp?PageID=84> (September 26, 2005).
2. Nicholas Tucker, *Inside the World of Philip Pullman: Darkness Visible* (New York: IBooks, 2003), p. 9.
3. Ibid., p. 11.
4. Philip Pullman, "From Exeter to Jordan," *Oxford Today*, 2002, <http://www.oxfordtoday.ox.ac.uk/archive/0102/14_3/03.shtml> (September 26, 2005).

Chapter 4. The Storytelling Teacher

1. Philip Pullman, "I Have A Feeling This All Belongs To Me," n.d., <http://www.philip-pullman.com/pages/content/index.asp?PageID=84> (September 26, 2005).

2. Nicholas Tucker, *Inside the World of Philip Pullman: Darkness Visible* (New York: IBooks, 2003), p. 19.

3. Ibid.

4. Pullman, "I Have A Feeling This All Belongs To Me."

5. Greta Stoddart, e-mail correspondence with author S. Reichard, May 2005.

6. Ibid.

Chapter 5. Heroes and Villians

1. Nicholas Tucker, *Inside the World of Philip Pullman: Darkness Visible* (New York: IBooks, 2003), p. 31.

2. Philip Pullman, "I Have A Feeling This All Belongs To Me," n.d., <http://www.philip-pullman.com/pages/content/index.asp?PageID=84> (September 26, 2005).

3. Ibid.

4. "Biobibliography—Philip Pullman," *The Astrid Lindgren Memorial Award*, n.d., <http://www.alma.se/page.php?realm=472> (January 23, 2006).

5. Tucker, p. 64.

6. Philip Pullman, "The Firework-Maker's Daughter," *Sheffield Theatres Education Resource*, March 2003, <http://www.sheffieldtheatres.co.uk/education/productions/fireworkmaker/pullman.shtml> (September 26, 2005).

7. "Theatre and Dance Previews: Philip Pullman's Aladdin and the Enchanted Lamp," *bbc.co.uk*, April 15, 2005, <http://www.bbc.co.uk/bristol/content/articles/2005/04/15/pullman_aladdin_feature.shtml> (January 25, 2006).

Chapter 6. The Books

1. Nicholas Tucker, *Inside the World of Philip Pullman: Darkness Visible* (New York: iBooks, 2003), pp. 55–56.

2. Ibid, p. 76.

3. Ibid, p. 48.

4. Ibid, p. 49.

5. Ann Moore, Editorial Review, *School Library Journal*, 1994, <http://www.amazon.com/execobidos/tg/detail/-/0679876154//ref=pd_bsgy?text> (November 5, 2004).

6. "The Firework-Maker's Daughter," *The Stage Online*, n.d., <http://www.thestage.co.uk/reviews/review.php/5655/the-fire-work-makers-daughter> (November 5, 2004).

7. Susan L. Rogers, Editorial Review, *School Library Journal*, n.d., <http://www.amazon.com/exec/obidos/tg/detail/-/> (November 5, 2004).

8. Patricia Dollisch, Editorial Review, *School Library Journal*, 1998, <http://www.amazon.com/exec/obidos/tg/detail/-/> (November 5, 2004).

9. "I Was a Rat!" Editorial Review, *Publisher's Weekly*, 1999, <http://www.amazon.com/exec/obidos/tg/detail/-/> (November 5, 2004).

10. John Peters, "Spring-Heeled Jack," Editorial Review, *School Library Journal*, 1991, <http://www.amazon.com/exec/obidos/tg/detail/-/044041881X//qid=1099657284> (November 5, 2004).

11. Gillian Engberg, Editorial Review, *Booklist*, n.d., <http://www.amazon.com/exec/obidos/tg/detail/-/0375813543//qid=1099657284> (November 5, 2004).

Chapter 7. Daemon's Darkness and Dust

1. Susan Bobby, "What Makes A Classic? Daemons and Dual Audience in Philip Pullman's *His Dark Materials*," *The Looking Glass*, December 9, 2004, vol. 8, p. 3.

2. Michael Chabon, "Dust and Demons," *The New York Review of Books*, October 4, 2004, <http://www.nybooks.com/articles/17000> (January 23, 2006).

3. Bobby, "What Makes A Classic?"

4. Nicholas Tucker, *Inside the World of Philip Pullman: Darkness Visible* (New York: iBooks, 2003), pp. 141–142.

5. Bobby, "What Makes A Classic?"

6. Waller Hasting, "Philip Pullman," n.d., <http://www.nothern.edu/hastingw/pullman.html> (November 5, 2004).

7. "Bridge To the Stars," n.d., <http://bridgeto thestars.net/index.php?d=encyclopedia> (November 5, 2004).

8. Philip Pullman, "Darkness Visible: An Interview with Philip Pullman (part 2)," n.d., <http://www.amazon.com> (November 5, 2004).

9. Tucker, p. 139.

10. Philip Pullman, *The Golden Compass* (N.Y.: Ballantine Books, 1995), pp. 349–350.

Chapter 8. Controversy and Critics

1. "BBC Interview with Philip Pullman," December 2003, <http://news.bbc.co. uk/cbbcnews/hi/uk/newsid3390000/ 339039.stm> (November 5, 2004).

2. Peter Hitchens, "This Is the Most Dangerous Author in Britain," *The Mail*, January 27, 2002, <http://pers-www.wlv.ac.uk/ ~bu1895/hitchens.htm> (January 24, 2006).

3. E-mail interview with Philip Pullman, conducted by author S. Reichard, October 2004.

4. Hitchens, "This Is the Most Dangerous Author in Britain."

5. John Cornwell, "Some Enchanted Author," *Times Online*, October 24, 2004, <http://www.timesonline.com/co.uk> (November 5, 2004).

6. Philip Pullman, "About the Writing," n.d., <http://www.philip-pullman.com.about_ the_writing.asp> (December 9, 2004).

7. Philip Pullman, "I Have A Feeling This All Belongs To Me," n.d., <http://www.philip-pullman.com/pages/content/index.asp?PageID=84> (September 26, 2005).

8. "The Art of Darkness," *Arts.telegraph*, November 11, 2004. <http://weather.telegraph.co.uk.arts.pg.1> (December 9, 2004).

9. Pullman, "About the Writing."

10. Philip Pullman, "Newsletter," March 11, 2005, <http://www.philip-pullman.com> (September 26, 2005).

11. "View on Religion," *Bridge to the Stars.net*, n.d., <http://www.bridgetothestars.net/index.php?d+commentaries/merlyn&p=part2> (January 23, 2006).

12. Ibid.

13. Sarah Lyall, "Philip Pullman: The Man Who Dared Make Religion the Villain," *The New York Times*, November 7, 2000, <http://www.nytimes.com/2000/11/07/arts/07PULL.html> (January 23, 2006).

14. "View on Religion," *Bridge to the Stars.net*.

15. Jorn Barger, "Philip Pullman Resources on the Web," *The Robot Wisdom Pages*, June 2002, <http://www.robotwisdom.com/jorn/pullman.html> (January 23, 2006).

16. "Daemon Geezer: Master of his Universe," Newsline: *The Online Newsletter of UCE Birmingham*, n.d., <http://www.uce.ac.uk/web2/newsline/pages/people47.html> (January 23, 2006).

Chapter 9. Success and Storytelling

1. Brunton, Michael, "You Don't Know How Famous You Are Until Complete Strangers Stop You In the Street to Talk," *Time Europe*, January 20, 2006, <http://www.time.com/time/europe/arts/printout/0,9869,579063,00.html> (January 23, 2006).

2. Newsround-BBC, "Pullman 'thrilled' by play of his books," January 2004, <http://news.bbc.co.uk/cbbcnews/hi/uk/newsid_3390000/3390039.stm> (January 23, 2006).

3. Email correspondence to author S. Reichard, Sept. 19, 2004.

4. Philip Pullman, "The Film," n.d., <http://www.philip-pullman.com/pages/content/index.asp?PageID=102> (January 23, 2006).

5. Robert Butler, *The Art of Darkness: Staging the Philip Pullman Trilogy* (London: Oberon Books, 2003), p. 31.

6. Philip Pullman, "About the Writing," n.d., <http://www.philip-pullman.com.about_the_writing.asp> (December 9, 2004).

7. Ibid.

8. Philip Pullman, "About the Books," n.d., <http://www.philip-pullman.com/pages/content/index.asp?PageID=90> (January 23, 2006).

9. Philip Pullman, "March Newsletter," March 2005, <http://www.philip-pullman.com/pages/content/index.asp?PageID=114> (March 17, 2005).

10. Ibid.

11. Philip Pullman, "New Year's Message," January 2006, <http://www.philip-pullman.com/pages/content/index.asp?PageID=120> (January 23, 2006).

Glossary

contemporary—Living or occurring in the same time period.

controversial—A debatable subject, a topic where different opinions exist.

epic—A long story about the deeds of a hero or heroes.

heresy—Religious beliefs opposed to the doctrines of a church. Any opinion opposed to the established views.

intercission—The act of cutting one's daemon (or demon) away; this is a neologism, or a new word, made up by Philip Pullman.

memorabilia—Things that are memorable and worth collecting.

oblation board—People who are in charge of providing a religious offering.

orthopedic—The branch of surgery dealing with bones and joints.

Queen Elizabeth II—The current monarch of England, who became queen in 1953.

subtle—Not obvious, not easily seen.

theme—A central subject or idea in a book or piece of writing.

trilogy—A set of three related books.

vagabond—One who lives a drifting or irresponsible life.

Victorian—Of the time of Queen Victoria.

Victorian England—Period of time in Great Britain from 1837–1901, when Victoria was queen.

Selected Works of Philip Pullman

FURTHER READING

Butler, Robert. *The Art of Darkness: Staging the Philip Pullman Trilogy.* London: Oberon Press, 2003.

Gribbin, Mary and John. *The Science of Philip Pullman's* His Dark Materials. New York: Knopf, 2005.

Lenz, Millicent, and Carde Scott, editors. *His Dark Materials Illuminated: Critical Essays on Philip Pullman's Trilogy.* Detroit: Wayne State University Press, 2005.

Tucker, Nicholas. *Darkness Visible: Inside the World of Philip Pullman.* New York: iBooks, 1992.

Wade, Mary Dodson. *C. S. Lewis: Chronicler of Narnia.* Berkeley Heights, N.J.: Enslow Publishers, Inc., 2005.

Watkins, Tony. *Dark Matter: A Thinking Fan's Guide to Philip Pullman.* Damaris Publications, 2004.

Internet Addresses

Official Philip Pullman Website
http://www.philip-pullman.com

Pullman's Publisher's Website
http://www.randomhouse.com/features/
pullman/philippullman/

His Dark Materials Fan Site
http://www.hisdarkmaterials.org

INDEX